NATIONAL GEOGRAPHIC LEARNING | **CENGAGE**

Weird BUT True!

- **2** **Strange Changes** *Science Article* by Barbara Keeler
- **10** **Freaky Features** *Science Article* by Barbara Keeler
- **18** **Spiders!** *Science Article* by Joe Baron
- **26** **Yellowstone in Flames** *Science Article* by Joe Baron
- **32** **Discuss**

GENRE Science Article

Read to find out about strange events and changes living things go through during their life cycles.

Strange Changes

by Barbara Keeler

Would you believe some plants survive by fooling animals? For example, the bee orchid is disguised to trick a male bumblebee! Like the bee orchid, all living things change as they grow. Some change a lot over the course of their **life cycle,** such as a grub-like caterpillar that develops into an adult butterfly with wings. Some change a little, such as a newly hatched alligator that looks like a miniature copy of its parents. Some living things go through surprising changes in how they look and how they live.

< Before blooming, the bee orchid buds look ordinary. After blooming, the orchid closely resembles an insect.

Fooled You!

The bee orchid, which grows in regions near the Mediterranean Sea, begins life as a seed and sprouts in soil. When the plant matures, flower buds form. Next comes a surprising transformation: when the flower blooms, it looks and smells like a female bumblebee! A passing male bumblebee can detect the odor and may land on the flower, mistaking it for a mate. When the male discovers the deception, it flies off, carrying some pollen. It then may **pollinate,** or drop pollen onto, another bee orchid. Once the bee orchid is pollinated, it can produce thousands of seeds.

Each bee orchid plant is unique. The plants with flowers that look and smell most like a female bumblebee are more likely to attract a pollinator, reproduce, and pass on their **traits,** or characteristics. This means that, over generations, bee orchids smell and look more and more like female bumblebees. And the male bumblebees continue to ensure there are plenty more bee orchids!

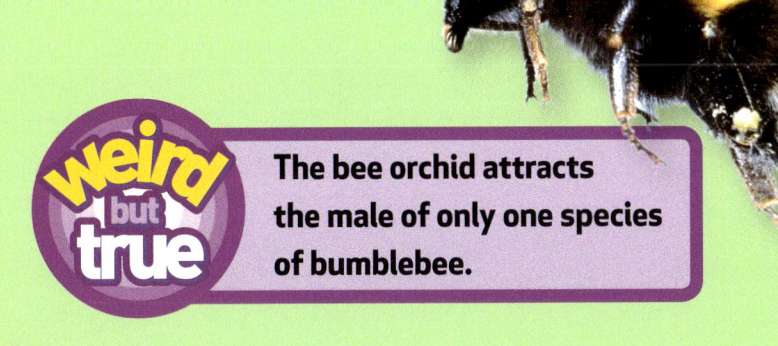

weird but true

The bee orchid attracts the male of only one species of bumblebee.

All Dung!

Ever think your meal is yucky? Be glad you're not a dung beetle. Not only do dung beetles eat dung, but they grow up in it! A dung beetle goes through extreme changes during its life cycle. What doesn't change is that it always is in or around animal dung!

Many dung beetles use their sense of smell to sniff out droppings of animals that eat plants. When they find the droppings, dinner is served! These droppings still contain undigested material with nutrients.

One kind of African dung beetle inherits an interesting behavior from its parents. Guided by instinct, it shapes dung into a ball and rolls it away. It buries the ball, either to snack on later or to lay eggs in. After the female lays an egg, a grub-like larva hatches and munches on the dung. Each larva molts, or sheds its **exoskeleton,** several times. It then enters the pupa stage, in which the insect's body parts undergo huge changes as it becomes an adult. The adult emerges from its cozy dung home and begins collecting and rolling dung on its own.

A Life of Dung

Egg

Larva

Pupa

Adult

Rather than being pests, dung beetles are beneficial to the environment. Large plant-eating animals produce huge amounts of dung. The dung beetles remove the waste and help it break down, releasing nutrients into the soil. For reducing the amount of waste that can attract disease-carrying flies, dung beetles get dung for dinner!

Weird but true

Dung Beetle Scoop

In one night, a dung beetle can bury as much as 250 times its own weight in dung.

Dung beetles that prefer fast food often try to steal another dung beetle's dung ball.

Dynamite Tree

Seeds from flowering plants are spread in different ways. The ways some seeds are spread are so dramatic you might call them explosive!

Growing in tropical America, from Mexico to Costa Rica, are some trees that you might want to avoid. Called sandbox trees, they are some of the tallest trees in the tropics. Sandbox trees can grow to about the height of a ten-story building. You might be attracted by the tree's spikes of flowers and pumpkin-shaped seed pods. Don't get too close, though—the seedpods can split suddenly, bursting open with a loud crack! The force of the scattering seeds can be enough to injure people or animals. Can you see why this tree has the nickname "dynamite tree"?

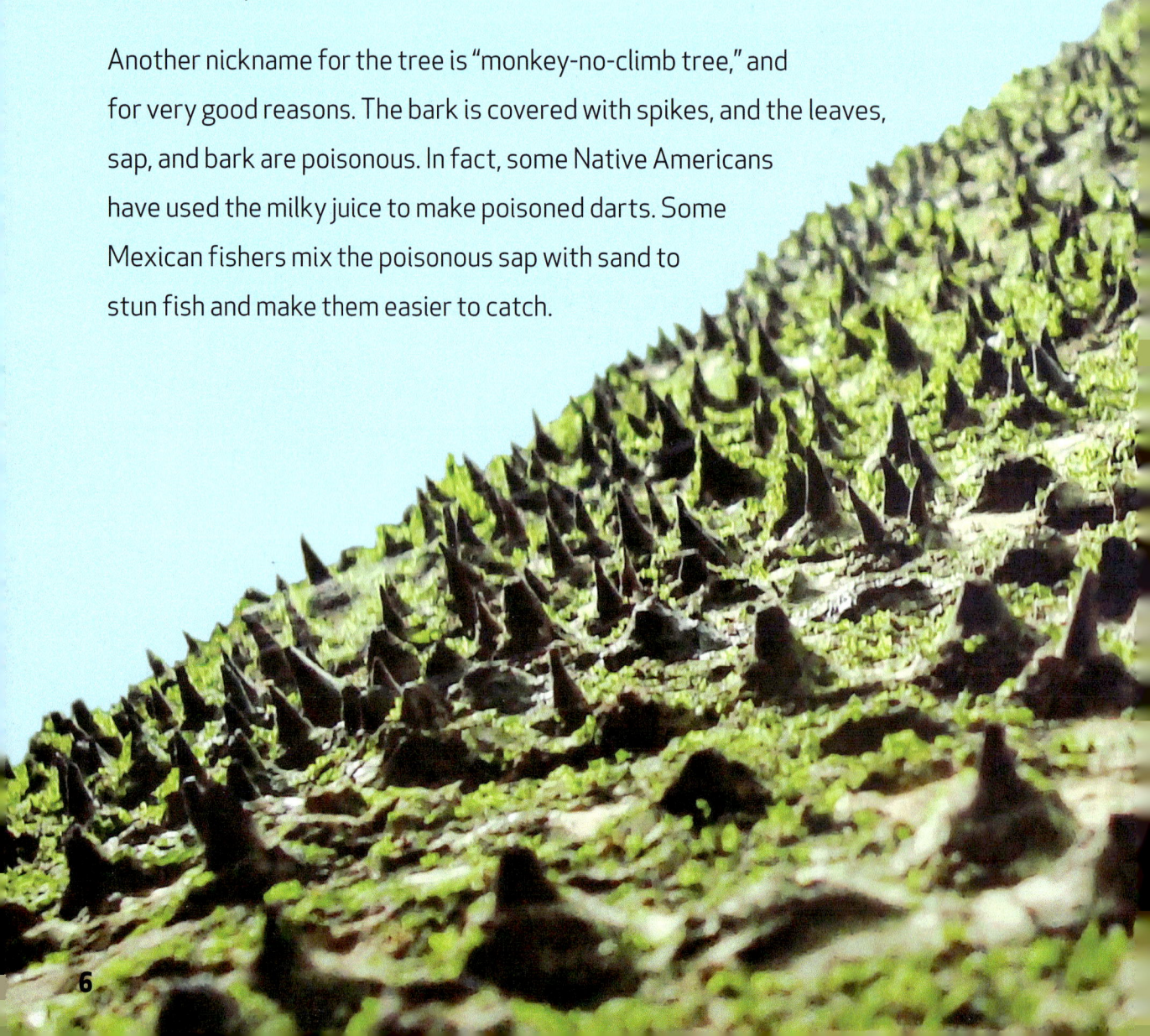

Another nickname for the tree is "monkey-no-climb tree," and for very good reasons. The bark is covered with spikes, and the leaves, sap, and bark are poisonous. In fact, some Native Americans have used the milky juice to make poisoned darts. Some Mexican fishers mix the poisonous sap with sand to stun fish and make them easier to catch.

weird but true

The seedpod of the sandbox tree can burst open with sudden force, scattering seeds for many meters.

7

See-Through Frog

Imagine a frog that looks like glass! The glass frog lives high in the trees in cloud forests of Central and South America. Like other frogs, the glass frog goes through tremendous changes during its life cycle. But the strangest feature of the glass frog is that its skin on the underside is nearly transparent. If you are looking up at the bottom of the frog, you can see the frog's internal organs! From above, its skin appears light green. These inherited traits make the frog seem to disappear as it sits on a leaf.

weird but true

Take a peek! You can observe the glass frog's heart beating. You might see food moving through its digestive system.

During the breeding season, the adult male and female glass frogs live in trees overhanging rivers and streams. The female lays eggs on the leaves, where they are safer than they would be in the predator-filled waters below. The male stays on the leaf to guard and care for the eggs. It protects the eggs from predators, such as frog flies, which try to lay eggs on the frog's eggs. If the flies succeed, their eggs hatch quickly and the larvae feed on the frog's eggs. If the frog's eggs dry out, they will not hatch, but the male has that problem solved. From time to time, he urinates on the eggs.

When the eggs hatch, the tadpoles drop into the water and begin to develop into adults. Once they are adults, the frogs return to the trees and the life cycle of this see-through frog begins again.

Eggs

Tadpole

Tadpole with limbs

Adult frog

< A glass frog begins life as an egg. It hatches as a tadpole. Over time, the tadpole grows limbs. Its tail gets shorter. Finally, it becomes an adult frog.

Check In Describe some traits of each plant and animal and some strange events and changes they go through during their life cycles.

9

GENRE Science Article **Read to find out** about adaptations that make animals look strange but help them survive in their environments.

Freaky Features

by Barbara Keeler

What has a body like a cross between pudding and gelatin that can stand up to tremendous pressure under water? It's the blobfish! The blobfish has **adaptations** that allow it to survive deep in the ocean. Adaptations are characteristics and behaviors that help organisms survive in their environments. These adaptations help animals move, feed, hide, reproduce, and survive dangers. Some organisms and their adaptations look—well—weird. You might even call them freaky! These organisms have inherited many adaptations from their parents. The parent organisms pass along **traits** to their offspring, so the young of many species look and behave like their parents.

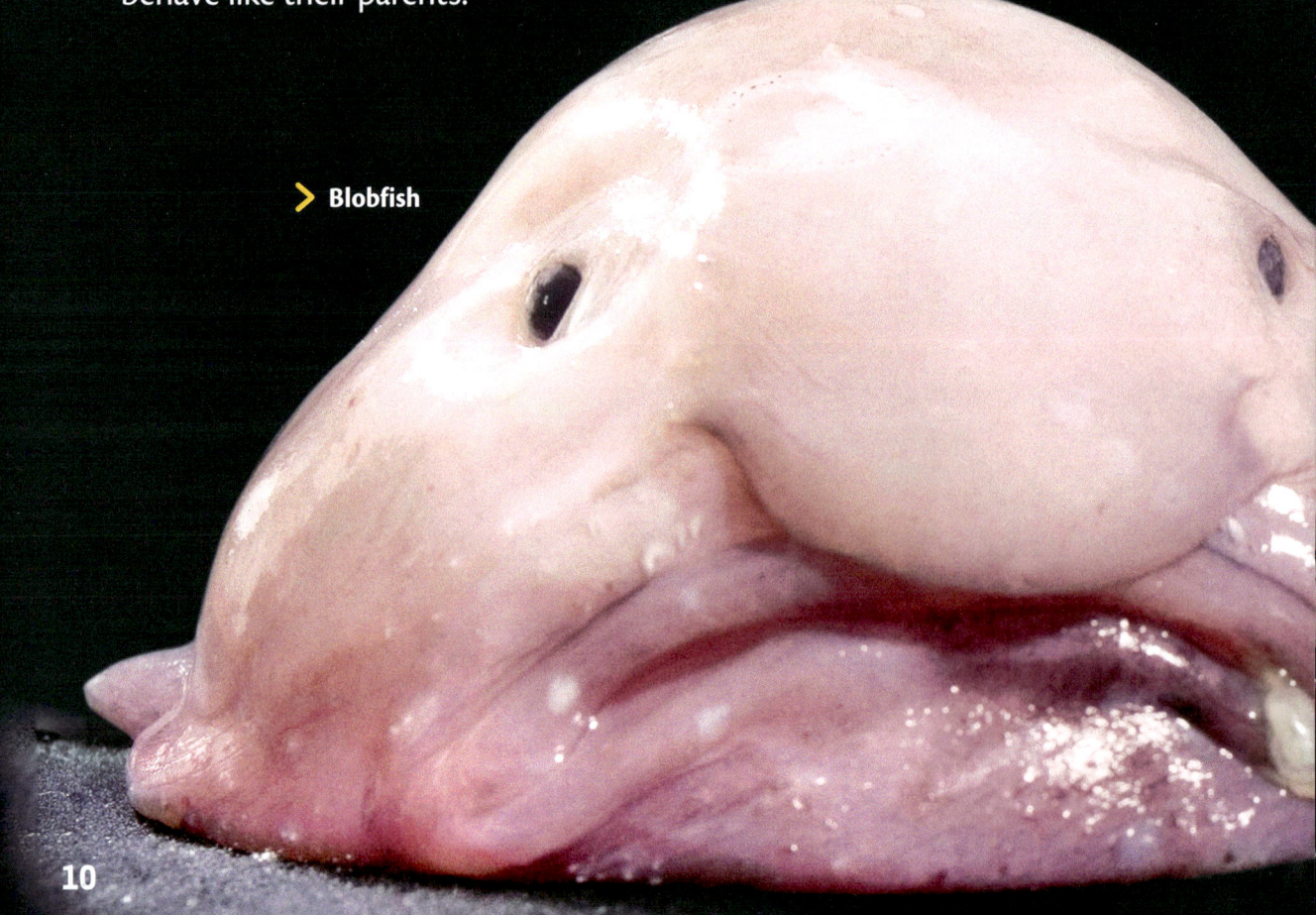

> Blobfish

Sea Monsters

It is no wonder people have reported sea monsters over the years. The ocean depths are home to some animals that look like creepy creatures in a horror movie.

The deep sea is not an easy place to live. Water temperatures may be close to freezing. It's dark, too. The deeper you go, the less sunlight you see, until light vanishes entirely. The deepest spot yet discovered lies approximately 11 kilometers (6.8 miles) below the surface.

The deeper you go, the greater the water pressure. Without special adaptations, a sea animal would be crushed like an egg shell. The blobfish is an example of a creature adapted to the deep ocean. Its blobby flesh is just right for holding up under the tremendous pressure.

Weird but true

The blobfish was only recently discovered. What looks like a nose is really a flap of blobby skin.

A Fish That Fishes

Even in the ocean depths, animals must eat and avoid being eaten. In a world without light, some "sea monsters" have chemicals that glow. Called **bioluminescence,** this characteristic helps some deep-sea beasts find prey.

The female deep sea anglerfish has a "fishing pole" on the end of its nose. Bacteria live at the tip and glow. Thinking the light is food, some fish swim toward it, only to be seized in fearsome jaws. Smaller than the female, a male anglerfish finds a female and latches on with its teeth. Over time the male and female become fused, and their blood vessels join. Whenever the female lays eggs, a male is handy to fertilize them.

⋀ The female anglerfish has a huge mouth. It can swallow prey twice its size. That is a good thing. The female's body may be feeding six or more males that have latched on.

Odd Octopus

Although octopuses have inherited some behaviors, they also learn new behaviors. For example, as they get older, they grow more alert to danger, showing that they learn from experience. They do not have very long to learn, however. Males die shortly after mating, and females die after their eggs hatch.

Highly intelligent, an octopus can solve mazes. It can also learn by watching another octopus. Scientists put two balls near an octopus, with a snack hidden behind one ball. It took that octopus a few tries to figure out which ball always had the snack behind it. Meanwhile, a second octopus watched the first octopus. When the second octopus was put near the balls, it found the snack on the first try and each time after. It had learned by watching the first octopus!

Octopuses are born looking like their parents—strange! The Dumbo octopus looks strange, even for an octopus. It has fins that look like the ears on the cartoon elephant with the same name.

Weird but true

An octopus is one of the most intelligent invertebrates. The giant Pacific octopus can learn to open a jar that contains prey.

Super Snouts

Land animals and water animals face different survival challenges. For example, under water, many animals can move by swimming alone. On land, other animals may need adaptations that help them run, crawl, dig in soil, climb, or fly to catch meals and avoid becoming meals themselves. They may need a fine sense of touch to find food. They may make sounds to communicate through the air. Some even use their noses in weird ways to survive!

With a world-class sniffer that is very sensitive to touch, the star-nosed mole uses the fleshy projections on its snout to locate small prey and to grab them with lightning speed. Found in northeastern United States and eastern Canada, the star-nosed mole has other adaptations for living on land. The broad, powerful forelimbs have huge claws for digging. Its poor eyesight is not a huge problem underground.

▽ The star-nosed mole has a snout with octopus-like projections. Can you count all 22 of them? Some are hard to see! The mole can identify and grab prey in about a quarter of a second.

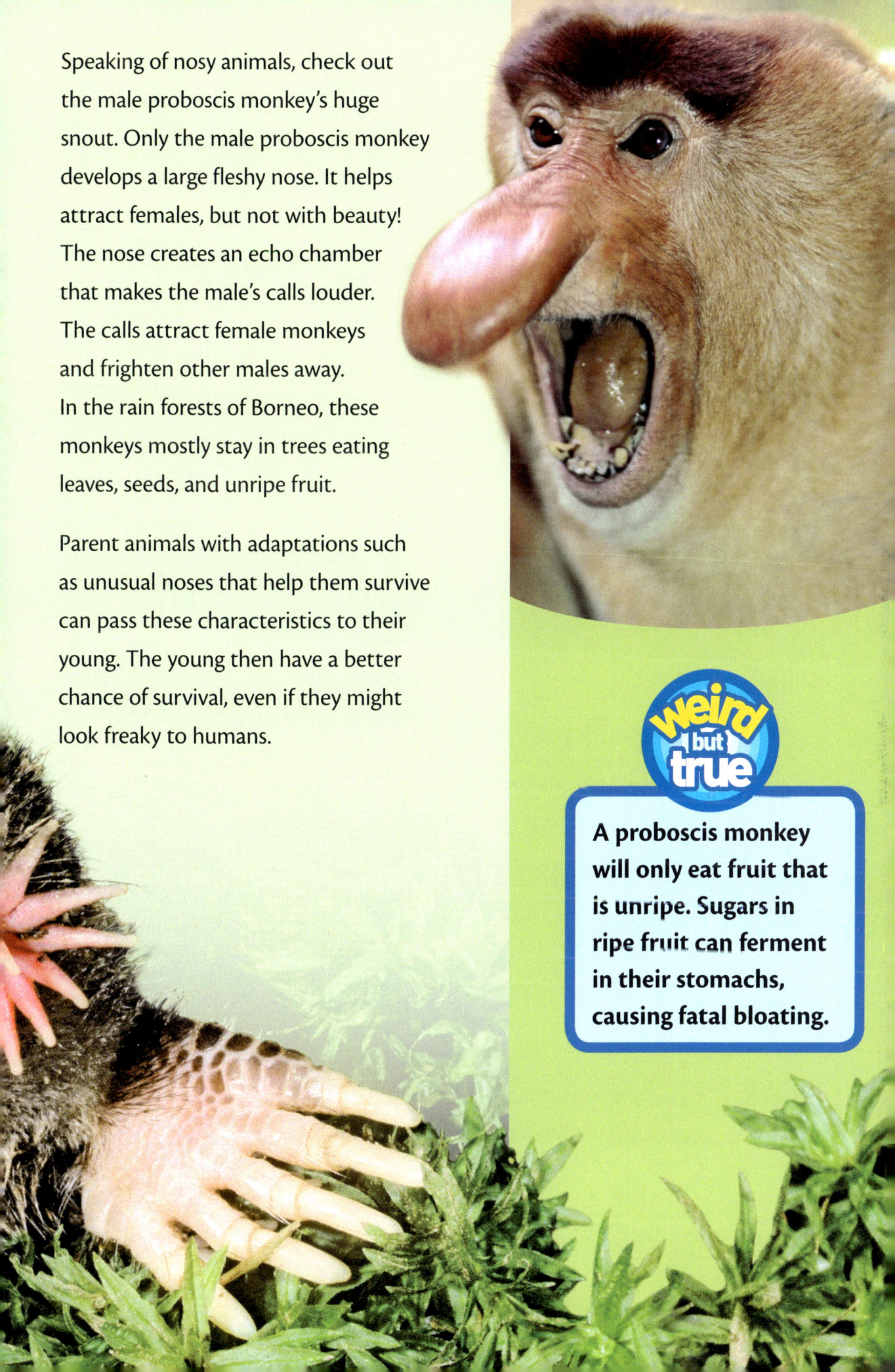

Speaking of nosy animals, check out the male proboscis monkey's huge snout. Only the male proboscis monkey develops a large fleshy nose. It helps attract females, but not with beauty! The nose creates an echo chamber that makes the male's calls louder. The calls attract female monkeys and frighten other males away. In the rain forests of Borneo, these monkeys mostly stay in trees eating leaves, seeds, and unripe fruit.

Parent animals with adaptations such as unusual noses that help them survive can pass these characteristics to their young. The young then have a better chance of survival, even if they might look freaky to humans.

weird but true

A proboscis monkey will only eat fruit that is unripe. Sugars in ripe fruit can ferment in their stomachs, causing fatal bloating.

Comeback Condors

Nobody would call condors cute, but the California condor is the largest flying bird in North America. Its body can be as long as 1.4 meters (4.5 feet) and its wing span nearly 3 meters (9.8 feet). The birds can glide on air currents as high as 4,600 meters (15,000 feet), or higher than the peaks of many mountains.

The California condor is the largest land bird of North America. A condor's huge wings allow it to soar on rising air currents that form when the sun heats the ground. It's kind of like a hang glider!

nearly 3 meters

Condors are scavengers that feast on carcasses of large mammals, such as cattle and deer. When enough food is available, the birds may stuff themselves so full that they must rest for hours before flying.

California condors were near extinction in the late 1970s. When their population dropped to very few individuals, scientists began a captive breeding program. Now, more than 100 birds live in the wild and are protected by law.

When the first human-raised condors were released, they did not figure out how to behave and survive in the wild. Many birds died, and others had to be captured again to keep them alive.

The young condors needed to learn from wild birds. Now, before releasing a young bird, biologists put out a carcass to attract wild condors. The young condor leaves its cage and joins the others at their feast. When the older birds fly off, the young one joins them.

From gooey blobfish deep in the ocean to bald-headed condors soaring high in the sky, many animals inherit some strange-looking adaptations. They may look freaky to us, but they suit these unusual animals just fine!

Weird but true

An adaptation such as a strong, sharp beak allows the condor to cut through tough animal hides. It must often stick its head into a carcass to reach the meat. A bald head can help the condor keep clean during meal time.

Check In What are some adaptations that animals inherit from their parents? What are some behaviors that some animals can learn?

GENRE Science Article **Read to find out** about spiders and how they make silk.

Spiders!

by Joe Baron

It has been said that you are rarely more than six feet from a spider. Most of the time, you probably do not see the spider, but the chances are the spider knows you are there. It has eight eyes and hairs all over its body to sense you and other objects. Although a few spiders are venomous, most are shy and seldom bite humans. Spiders come in many shapes and colors and can be as small as a pencil point or as big as a dinner plate.

A female spider lays eggs in a silk egg sac. A few weeks later, they hatch as spiderlings that closely resemble their parents. Spiderlings molt, or shed their **exoskeletons,** several times as they grow, and become adults after one year.

A spider has two main body parts. One is its head region. The other is a back section called the abdomen.

A spider has eight eyes.

The whole spider is covered with hair. The hairs help a spider sense nearby objects.

Like other arachnids, a spider has eight legs.

Two stubby limbs stick out from the head region. Spiders use them like hands.

Spiders' jaws end in sharp fangs. Each fang has a tiny hole that releases venom.

Wide World of Webs

The abdomen of a spider contains organs that help spiders do something special: make silk. Spider silk begins as a fluid oozing from the abdomen. Air turns the fluid into tough fiber. In fact, some spiders make silk that is stronger than steel of the same thickness. Spiders use their silk to tie up prey. They make silk draglines, or threads that keep a spider from falling. Females wrap silk around their eggs. Some spiders even make silk "parachutes" to sail off and find new homes. They also use it to solve the problem of getting food. Spiders weave many kinds of webs. They always use their webs to catch prey.

Some spiders make orb webs that look like wheels with spokes. Building one takes at least an hour. Then the spider waits in the middle. An insect flies into the sticky threads. The spider jumps into action, racing over and injecting the prey with venom to paralyze or kill it.

Labyrinth spiders do things differently. They weave a web with a flat surface that narrows into a tube-like shelter. When an insect lands on the web, the spider darts out and snatches it with a bite. Then the spider drags the prey inside for dinner.

▲ Sheetweb spiders weave flat webs that stretch across bushes or grassy fields.

▼ Net-casting spiders make small silk nets. They toss their nets over prey to catch dinner.

weird but true

The Spin on Spiders

A spider's stomach is in its head region.

A spider smells and tastes with its feet.

Spider venom is used in medicine.

If you unwound one of the largest spider webs, the silk would stretch out 480 kilometers (300 miles)!

Some kinds of spiders eat other spiders.

About 37,000 kinds of spiders live on Earth.

In South America, people eat roasted tarantulas!

Frogs, toads, lizards, birds, mice, beetles, wasps, and centipedes prey on spiders.

21

Wild Without Webs

Spiders aren't picky eaters. Bees, flies, moths—they're all good. Tarantulas even eat mice and small birds. Once a spider catches prey, it has a problem to solve. A spider can't chew or swallow, so how will it eat its prey? The spider injects juices to make the prey's insides soupy, then slurps them up.

Speaking of catching prey, only about half of the world's spiders spin webs. How does the other half catch dinner? They have their ways!

› Trap-door spiders live in holes. They make doors out of silk and dirt. At night a spider raises the door and sticks its head out. It grabs anything edible that walks by.

› Wolf spiders, crab spiders, and tarantulas are stalkers. They hunt other critters. A wolf spider is shown devouring a cricket.

⌄ Jumping spiders sneak up and pounce on tasty-looking animals. The spider spins a dragline to prevent it from falling if it misses its prey.

Dig In and Devour

All the eating spiders do adds up. Arachnologists, scientists who study spiders, might explore ways to learn just how much spiders actually eat.

One research team, for example, studied spiders living on an acre of farmland. Added together, spiders there ate about 34 kilograms (75 pounds) of insects each day. That's about the weight of 750 hot dogs!

Spiders do not eat only insects. Some of the larger ones eat frogs, small snakes, lizards, mice, and bats. In fact, the Goliath bird-eating tarantula even eats birds. As you might guess, this spider is huge! Its body can grow to be about 9 centimeters (3.5 inches) long and its leg span can be over 25 centimeters (about 10 inches). It sneaks up, seizes its prey, and then kills it with the venom in its fangs.

Maybe because of their eight eyes and hairy legs, or maybe because they seem to creep and crawl out of nowhere—spiders seem to have earned a bad reputation. But without spiders' big appetites, we would be sharing the planet with many more insects. In fact, next time you see a spider, you might find a reason to smile!

⌄ Goliath bird-eating tarantula

Weird but true

Happy Face Spider

Native to Hawai'i, the happy face spider measures only a few millimeters across. The spider's markings may discourage birds from eating it. The female sits on a leaf, guarding her eggs that are laid in an egg sac. Unlike most spiders, she cares for her young. She even captures prey for the spiderlings to eat. Now that's something to smile about!

Check In What are some adaptations of spiders that help them survive?

25

GENRE Science Article | **Read to find out** how the worst fire in Yellowstone's history affected wildlife.

Yellowstone in Flames

by Joe Baron

The summer of 1988 was the driest in Yellowstone National Park's recorded history. The parched grasses and dried leaves in the forests of western Wyoming had become a tinderbox waiting to ignite. While fires had occurred many times in the park, the 1988 drought had set the stage for a spectacular and ferocious fire. All that was needed was a trigger.

A few small fires started in June. By August and September, lightning storms with no rain set some fires, and careless people set others. Soon, fires raged through the park. Trees crackled and exploded into flames that towered over the forest. The heat of the fire increased the speed and force of the winds. Driven by fierce winds, flames leaped from one place to another. Animals raced for their lives.

Although more than 25,000 people worked to fight the fire, firefighters had little impact on the inferno. Rain and snow finally began to fall in September. Weeks later, the fire was over.

The voracious appetites of the flames left vast areas of the park charred and smoldering. Many people thought a national treasure had been lost. Most did not expect the forest to **regenerate,** or regrow, soon. They worried about how the park would look for the next generation of visitors. What do you think you would see if you visited the park in the days or weeks after the fire? How would you feel?

YELLOWSTONE FIRE FACTS

The fire affected more than 36% of the park.

Fires that began outside of the park burned more than half the total acreage.

Lightning caused 42 fires, and humans caused 9 fires.

About 300 large mammals, mostly elk, died, but more than 30,000 elk survived.

The cost of fighting the fire was $120 million.

Although the huge fire-fighting effort had little impact on the fires themselves, it saved human life and property.

The cones of a lodgepole pine tree are sealed by sap until the heat of a fire cracks them to release the seeds and grow new trees. Fire helps new trees grow!

weird but true

After the Flames

Many people did not understand that fire plays an important role in the park's ecosystem. Elk and bison, however, behaved as though they recognized fire as a natural occurrence. According to a ranger, when a fire front approached, the animals fled the forest into a large open area. There, they grazed or waited until the fire front had passed. Then many of them headed right back into the burned areas.

As it turns out, fire is not all bad in the park. In fact, many living things have **adaptations** that allow them to survive and thrive after a major fire! Over thousands of years, plants with **traits** that adapted them to fire survived and reproduced, passing the adaptations on.

YELLOWSTONE FIRE FACTS

By changing the mineral balance, ash made the soil more fertile. Some plants grew rapidly in the spring after the fire.

Grasslands returned to their pre-fire conditions within a few years.

After a fire, it can take more than 100 years for lodgepole pines to reach maturity. Mature trees reach heights of between 18 to 25 meters (about 60 to 80 feet).

Bears grazed more frequently at burned than unburned sites.

The fires did not seem to reduce the number of grizzly bears in greater Yellowstone.

Bluebirds and other birds that build nests in holes in trees had more dead trees for their nests. However, birds that depend on live, fully grown trees lost places to live.

For example, lodgepole pines, which make up nearly 80% of the park's forests, are adapted to regenerate after a fire. Aspen trees are also adapted to fire. The fires triggered the growth of suckers, or new sprouts, from the aspen's underground roots. The bare mineral soil left behind from the fire improved conditions for aspen seedlings. Douglas fir trees have very thick bark that protects them and insulates them against heat. Mature Douglas fir trees usually survive a fire.

Yellowstone Today

Park scientists learned from past fires, including the fire in 1988. Until the 1970s, most park managers believed they had to put out all fires to preserve park resources. Scientific research changed these beliefs. For example, scientists learned that suppressing all fire reduces the number and variety of plant and animal species. In 1972, Yellowstone managers began allowing most fires to burn if they started from natural causes. They continued to fight human-caused fires and to protect homes and towns from fires. The 1988 fires brought new opportunities for research that resulted in further management changes.

After observing some advantages to forest burning and regeneration, park mangers began to practice controlled burning. They actually started and controlled fires! Controlled burning can help the forest in these ways:

- reduce dangerous buildup of growth that could fuel large fires;
- manage plants that compete with and crowd out others;
- control plant diseases;
- improve the survival of species that depend on fire; and
- put nutrients in the soil.

As terrifying as fires can be, and as destructive as they may be in the short term, many plants and animals depend on fire. It has taken humans centuries to learn what the bison and elk seemed to know by instinct. Fire is a natural part of the Yellowstone ecosystem. In fact, if nature does not provide a fire when or where one is needed, humans are now giving nature some help! Park workers now manage carefully controlled fires to help preserve the natural conditions in Yellowstone National Park.

Scientists and visitors have a new appreciation for the wonders of Yellowstone. Today, controlled fires help keep Yellowstone a great place for wildlife and tourists alike.

YELLOWSTONE FIRE FACTS

Large fires burn through forests of Yellowstone every 250–400 years.

Large fires burn the park's grasslands every 25–60 years.

Lightning starts an average of 22 fires each year.

About 80% of naturally started fires go out by themselves.

Check In How are some different plants adapted to survive and reproduce after a fire?

Discuss

1. What connections can you make among the four pieces in the book? How are the pieces related?

2. In "Strange Changes," you read about several life cycles. Compare and contrast the life cycles of the dung beetle and the glass frog.

3. Think about and describe three inherited adaptations of animals in "Freaky Features." How does each adaptation help the animal survive?

4. Compare and contrast the ways one web-spinning spider and one spider that does not spin a web capture food.

5. What do park workers do to prevent unusually large forest fires?

6. What do you still wonder about ways that animals and plants are adapted to survive in their environments? What research can you do to find out more?